SPY SECRETS

Copyright © 2007 Top That! Publishing plc
Tide Mill Way, Woodbridge, Suffolk, IP12 1AP, UK
www.topthatpublishing.com
Top That! Kids is a trademark of Top That! Publishing plc

The world of spying is exciting and dangerous, full of great rewards for success but the cruellest of punishments for failure.

Fiction

Most of us only know about espionage from books and films such as the James Bond series, where 007 usually saves the world with only a few seconds to spare before falling into the arms of a beautiful woman. Before the end of the film, he has usually managed to escape from the clutches of an evil genius threatening him with some hideous torture.

Fact

The truth about spies is rather different. Unlike James Bond they are not always motivated by loyalty to their country. Some are bullied to spy, others are motivated by money. While their work is full of adventure, if they are caught red-handed they do not miraculously escape. They are more likely to be sent to prison for many years, or in some cases sentenced to a horrible death.

History

Spying is often described as one of the world's oldest professions. Indeed, there are stories of espionage in the Bible. In *Spy Secrets* you'll find out all about the dangerous things spies have done, from biblical times to the present day, and you'll find out about some of the amazing equipment they have used in their work.

Daniel Craig as James Bond in the film Casino Royale
UNITED ARTISTS/SONY PICTURES

What is a Spy?

Spies can be roughly divided into four groups: intelligence agents, counterintelligence agents, industrial spies and double agents.

Intelligence

Intelligence work involves gathering information about the military and political affairs of other countries. However, this does not mean just reading the newspapers published in that country; a spy's job is to gain information that another country does not want to be found out. Therefore, the spy's work must always be done in secret and will often involve breaking the law.

Kim Philby worked for MI5, but spied for the Russians.

Counterintelligence

Counterintelligence agents gather information on enemy spies. You might think that once a spy has been caught he or she should be arrested, but espionage is rarely that simple. After all, if the spy was arrested your enemy would then try to replace them and you would need to identify the replacement. A counter intelligence agent will feed false information to the spy so that the secrets they betray are either untrue or of little value.

Double Agents

Most spies are loyal to their country, but some are not. They pretend to spy for Country A, but in reality they are providing useless information while secretly giving valuable information to Country B. As they are trusted by Country A they often have access to highly classified information. Employed by the British agency MI5, Kim Philby was, in fact, spying for the Russians.

Industrial Espionage

Some companies use industrial espionage in order to find out their competitors' plans. They may pay an employee to get a job with the target company or they may blackmail or bribe an existing employee to provide information. Although this is illegal, some companies will take the risk because it saves them money – instead of spending huge sums of money on research they just steal someone else's.

Spy Tools

Spies use the latest technology to help them track their target. Miniature cameras have been used for decades to capture secret documents and take photos undercover. Another useful piece of equipment is the mobile phone, which can now take pictures and videos and send information immediately all over the world via satellites.

Intelligence Organisations

All of the most powerful countries in the world use intelligence organisations to protect themselves, both from internal and external threats.

MI5 and MI6

MI (Military Intelligence) 5 and MI6 are the two arms of British intelligence. MI5 looks after the internal security of the country and is responsible directly to the Prime Minister. MI6 is responsible for spying on other countries and is largely under the control of the Foreign Office. Electronic surveillance is carried out by GCHQ (Government Communications Headquarters), at the request of MI5 and MI6.

The CIA and FBI

The CIA (Central Intelligence Agency) and FBI (Federal Bureau of Investigation) are responsible for American intelligence. The FBI is charged with domestic security and the CIA with foreign policy operations. The CIA is a

George Bush Snr.

controversial body as it has often had the task of deliberately undermining foreign governments, particularly in Central

MI6 Headquarters.

Intelligence Organisations

America, in order to protect American financial interests. George Bush, the former president and father of President George W Bush, was once head of the CIA.

The KGB

The KGB (Committee of State Security), responsible for spying in the Soviet Union, was one of the most notorious intelligence agencies of the 20th century. When the Soviet Union collapsed in the early 1990s, the KGB was replaced by the FSB (Federal Security Service).

Cruel Punishment

The communist policies pursued by the Soviet government were unpopular with many people and so KGB spies were ordered to watch out for any signs of rebellion. Anybody caught encouraging anti-government sentiment would be sent to prison

Vladimir Putin.

or exiled to Siberia, one of the coldest places in the world. In fact, many of these people mysteriously disappeared. The current president of Russia, Vladimir Putin, worked for the KGB in the 1970s and 1980s, and was head of the FSB before becoming president.

Olympic champion Katarina Witt.

Mossad

Mossad is responsible for intelligence and counter intelligence for the Israeli government. For some time there has been a great deal of tension between Israel, a mostly Jewish country, and the mainly Muslim Arab states, and so Mossad is a very active organisation.

The Stasi

The Stasi, the East German secret police organisation, was also notorious. People were often blackmailed or bribed to inform on their own family. Many people believe that Katarina Witt, who won an Olympic gold medal in ice skating in 1984, was forced to become a spy by the Stasi. When the Cold War ended, East Germany united with West Germany in 1990 and the Stasi was then dissolved.

Early Days

Spying is one of the oldest professions in the world. Even in biblical times, people sought advantage over one another by underhand means.

Samson and Delilah

The story of Samson and Delilah is told in the Bible. Samson, an incredibly strong man, was a hero of Israel in the country's battles against the Philistines. The Philistines offered Delilah 1,000 pieces of silver to spy for them. Her mission was to help the Philistines capture Samson.

A still from Cecil B. DeMille's film Samson and Delilah *(1949) starring Hedy Lamarr and Victor Mature.*

Tricked

Delilah tricked Samson into revealing that the key to his strength was his hair, and that if it was cut he would become weak. When Samson was asleep, Delilah cut his hair and called some Philistine soldiers to take him away. The Philistines blinded him and chained him to the pillars in the temple. In a final act of strength, Samson shook the pillars free, causing the temple to collapse. Everybody inside, including Delilah and Samson himself, was killed.

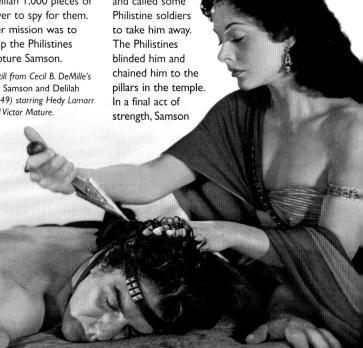

Francis Walsingham

Francis Walsingham was the spymaster for his queen, Elizabeth I, in the 16th century. Elizabeth, a Protestant queen, was

An engraving of spymaster Francis Walsingham.

deeply distrustful of Catholics, who she believed, often rightly, were seeking to overthrow and replace her with the Catholic Mary, Queen of Scots. After the plot to overthrow Elizabeth was revealed, Mary was executed in 1587.

Spanish Invasion

Mary's execution contributed to the decision of King Philip II of Spain to send his fleet of ships, the Armada, to invade England in 1588. Walsingham had foreseen that this might happen and had spies swarming over the Spanish coast. The spies were able to send vital information about the time the Armada was leaving and which route it was taking.

Cardinal Richelieu

Cardinal Richelieu was the great French spymaster of the 17th century. He secretly encouraged Sweden to fight an expensive war with the Austro-Hungarian empire, in order to weaken the power of both states.

Spy Network

French nobles were jealous of Richelieu's popularity and were always plotting against him. Richelieu knew this and employed a vast network of spies to protect him.

Alexander the Great

Alexander the Great, King of Macedonia during the 3rd century BC, spied on his own soldiers. While at war in Asia Minor, Alexander decided he needed to know which of his soldiers he could trust. After his troops wrote to their families at home, Alexander's men intercepted the couriers delivering the letters. The letters were checked, and Alexander then knew which of his soldiers were loyal.

Casanova and Paul Revere are legendary historical figures; Casanova as a great lover and Revere as an American hero. However, few people know they were both spies.

Casanova – a spy known for his romantic liaisons.

Charmer

During the Seven Years' War (1856–63), Casanova was asked to work out the strength of the British fleet stationed at Dunkirk. He used his great charm to persuade the captains of the British ships to invite him aboard for dinner. To avoid suspicion he only questioned the more trusting younger officers about the Navy's strength. Although Louis XV was impressed by Casanova's work, the war ended in defeat for France.

Casanova

Although 18th-century Italian adventurer Casanova is better known for his romantic liaisons, he was also a spy for the French king, Louis XV. Said to be a charming man who liked to gamble and perform magic tricks, Casanova only spied when he was short of money.

Paul Revere

Paul Revere, hero of the American War of Independence, was the head of a secret society that spied on the British. In 1775 British troops were sent to Lexington in Virginia to arrest the rebel leaders John Hancock and Samuel Adams, but when they arrived they were attacked by armed farmers known as minutemen.

Coded Warning

How did the minutemen know the British were coming? Revere had received a coded warning from one of his spies in Boston and had then ridden through the night to Lexington to warn them. Although the Battle of Lexington

An engraving of the Duke of Wellington.

was really no more than a skirmish, it led to further battles and eventually the American Declaration of Independence, on 4th July 1776.

Henry Hardinge

Henry Hardinge was the Duke of Wellington's spymaster during the Napoleonic wars at the start of the 19th century. He persuaded a network of Spanish soldiers fighting for Napoleon to provide information to the British army. Wellington's famous victory at the Battle of Waterloo might well have been a defeat had it not been for Hardinge's discovery of some of the details of Napoleon's secret battle plans.

Baden-Powell

Robert Baden-Powell, best known as the founder of the Scout Association, was a true hero. Before World War One many people believed that war might break out in the Balkans, a mountainous area of Europe. Baden-Powell travelled around one of the Balkan states, Herzegovina, pretending to catch butterflies. In reality he was going as near to enemy fortresses as he dared in order to draw maps of their defences. The drawings were hidden inside his sketches of butterflies and then smuggled back to British forces.

The 20th century saw the two largest-scale wars of all time. Of course, this meant that spies were in more demand than ever before.

Mata Hari.

Mata Hari

Dutchwoman Mata Hari is one of the most famous spies of all time. However, this does not mean she was particularly good at her job – after all, nobody has ever heard of the best spies because their work remains a secret. Before World War One Hari was one of the most popular dancers in Paris, so when the war began she was in a good position to become a spy because she knew so many important people.

Double Agent?

Mata Hari sold secrets to the German forces, but when the French discovered she was a spy she made a deal, offering to change sides. However, Mata Hari did not keep her part of the bargain and continued to work for the Germans, only pretending to spy for France. At her trial she denied spying for the Germans, claiming that all her work had been for France. She was found guilty and shot as a traitor.

Beria

Russian spymaster Lavrenti Beria was one of the most evil men

Lavrenti Beria.

of the 20th century. Following the Russian revolution, Beria began his spying career by informing on friends and relatives who questioned the government's communist policies. Beria was promoted to higher and higher posts within the secret police, but the vacancy usually appeared after Beria had blackmailed the jobholder.

Ruthless

Nothing was allowed to stand in Beria's way; if people could not be blackmailed he would have them murdered. Eventually he rose to become head of the NKVD (the forerunner to the KGB), a very influential position in Stalin's Russia. Eventually Beria fell victim to the one problem spies frequently encounter – nobody, including people on his own side, trusted him. In 1953, shortly after Stalin's death, Beria was executed as a traitor.

Joseph Stalin ruled the Soviet Union.

Lawrence of Arabia

Lawrence of Arabia (real name: Thomas Edward Lawrence) was sent to work for army intelligence in North Africa in1914. He disguised himself as an archaeologist in order to make maps of the area. His knowledge of the area, then controlled by the Turks, was to prove crucial to the successful Arab revolt as he knew which positions were vulnerable. Lawrence's exploits and his book, *The Seven Pillars of Wisdom*, made him famous.

World War Two Spies

During World War Two, the war fought by Britain and its Allies against Hitler's Nazi Germany, espionage reached new levels of sophistication. One spy even saw his name enter the language.

Quisling

Norwegian politician Vidkun Quisling was leader of the country's Fascist party. He helped Hitler by telling him how his ships should navigate the fjords of

Vidkun Quisling.

Norway and persuaded friends in the army not to resist the German invasion. He was so successful that the Germans took over Norway virtually unopposed. A grateful Hitler then appointed Quisling prime minister of Norway.

Hated

Most Norwegians despised Quisling and the way in which he had helped Hitler. When the war ended in Germany's defeat, Quisling was shot as a traitor. Anyone who betrays their country and aids an occupying force is now described as a quisling.

Josephine Baker

Josephine Baker was an American singer and dancer working in Paris when war broke out. Originally she joined the Red Cross before working for the French resistance movement. She was able to obtain information about German plans because many high-ranking Germans would come to see her perform at her club. By observing the Germans carefully and talking to them, she was able to pick up valuable titbits of information about their plans and discover which Frenchmen were working for the enemy.

*Jose
Bak
wo
for
Fre
res*

World War Two Spies

Odette Sansom (second from left) and Peter Churchill.

Churchill was the nephew of British Prime Minister Winston Churchill (they shared the same surname, but were unrelated). The Germans believed the couple and so treated them leniently.

Mme. Sansom

Odette Sansom was a Frenchwoman living in London in 1939. She longed to play an active part in the war and so became an undercover courier for the Special Operations Executive. In 1942 she was sent to southern France where her role was to act as a radio operator and contact for British spy Peter Churchill.

Betrayed

In 1943, Sansom and Churchill were betrayed by a French double agent. Interrogated and tortured, neither revealed a single British secret. In fact, they pretended that they were married and that

Ian Fleming

Better known as the author of the James Bond stories, Ian Fleming was a British spy during World War Two. He joined British Naval Intelligence in 1939 and helped to co-ordinate joint British and American operations. In 1944 he commanded a Royal Marines unit in France, charged with capturing enemy codes and weapons. His code name was not 007, but 17F.

Codebreaking in World War Two

Although victory in war requires immense bravery, it's of little use if you have the wrong information. It has long been recognised that the breaking of the Enigma code was crucial to the Germans' defeat.

The Enigma machine.

Enigma

The Enigma machine encoded all German naval communications. The job of cracking the codes was given to the Government Code and Cipher School (GCCS), based at Bletchley Park in Buckinghamshire. Enigma was finally cracked by Alan Turing in early 1941. British intelligence officers were then able to listen in to German orders to their ships and U-boats (submarines). In 1942, however, the Germans made a small alteration to the Enigma machine and, once again, the codebreakers were clueless and the British began to sustain huge losses at sea.

Crucial Mistake

It was only when the Germans made a mistake in 1943 that the Enigma code was solved once again.

A German U-boat.

Codebreaking in World War Two

Bletchley Park, where the GCCS was based.

Two messages were sent, one fully coded and one where the coding was incomplete. This enabled Turing and his colleagues to work out what each letter meant. From this point on the Germans were hopelessly disadvantaged at sea. Whatever plans they made for their navy, the Allied forces always knew what they were going to do.

Lorenz Machine

The codebreakers at Bletchley Park were not just concerned with breaking the codes of the Enigma machine, there was

also the Lorenz machine, used by the most important German generals for their top-secret communications. The Lorenz machine was linked to a teleprinter, which converted messages into patterns of punched holes on paper tape. The machine was cracked by

William Tutte and, as with the Enigma, the solving of the code proved decisive to the Germans' eventual defeat.

Colossus

The solving of the Enigma and Lorenz codes got the scientists and mathematicians at Bletchley thinking about electronic codes and led directly to the invention of the first electronic computer, known as Colossus. The computers we use today might not exist without the invention and solution of wartime codes.

The first electronic computer, Colossus

The Cold War

After World War Two, the biggest threat to world peace was the tension that built between the United States and the Soviet Union and their Allies. The period from the mid-1940s to the early 1990s was known as the Cold War. Although these two superpowers didn't get on, they never actually fought one another.

Destructive Force

Both the United States and the Soviet Union had access to nuclear weapons, which, if used, would have caused destruction on an absolutely massive scale.

Nuclear Deterrent

Since neither side wanted to be responsible for causing total devastation, these nuclear weapons acted as a deterrent to starting a war.

Top Secret

The Manhattan Project was the name of the top-secret programme to develop a nuclear bomb. Begun in Britain in 1940, it was transferred to America in 1941. The project was proved successful in 1945 when two bombs were dropped on Japan, but the KGB's spies had already found out about the project and wanted to discover how the bomb worked.

The explosion created by a nuclear bomb causes total devastation.

Klaus Fuchs

German-born Klaus Fuchs was a very talented scientist living

Klaus Fuchs.

in Britain during World War Two. Suspected of being a German spy, he was eventually trusted enough to be sent to America to work on the Manhattan Project.

No one knew that he was already spying for the Soviet Union. There is no doubt that Fuchs' work was of enormous help to the Soviets' nuclear bomb development programme.

Caught

When he was finally caught, Fuchs claimed that he had given away the project's secrets because he believed peace was more likely if both sides had the bomb. This may be true since Fuchs refused Soviet offers of payment for his work.

The Rosenbergs

Julius Rosenberg and his wife Ethel were also spies working at Los Alamos, where the Manhattan Project took place. Their cover was blown by Fuchs' capture, and they were sentenced to death in 1951. They are notorious as the first American citizens to be executed for espionage.

Cold War Flashpoints

There were several occasions in the Cold War when war seemed inevitable. Espionage was usually involved somewhere.

The Cuban Missile Crisis

In 1962, American spy planes flying over Cuba revealed that sites for launching nuclear missiles were being built in the country.

Che Guevara played a key role in the Cuban Missile Crisis.

Cuba was near enough for the Americans to feel threatened. After following Cuban industry minister Che Guevara to the Russian capital, Moscow, the CIA was certain that the sites were being built for the Soviets. The American president, John F. Kennedy, demanded that the sites be dismantled, but his Russian counterpart, Nikita Khrushchev, refused. Eventually Khrushchev backed down, but for a while it seemed that war was inevitable.

The Assassination of President Kennedy

When President Kennedy was shot dead in Dallas in 1963 it was soon discovered that the man accused of killing him, Lee Harvey Oswald, had spent time in the Soviet Union.

The Americans suspected that Oswald was a KGB agent, and the Russians were afraid that the Americans would believe it.

Nosenko

Shortly after the assassination, a KGB agent, Yuri Nosenko, arrived in America claiming that he wanted to change sides and that he had valuable information about Oswald. He claimed that the KGB had not tried to recruit Oswald because he was mentally unstable. The CIA did not believe Nosenko, thinking that his story was too neat and was intended to make them believe that the KGB had nothing to do with Kennedy's assassination.

Lee Harvey Oswald is thought to have been responsible for the assassination of President Kennedy.

Caged

Nosenko was kept in cruel conditions for three years in a tiny cell, lit by a single lightbulb. Despite being tortured, he stuck to his story. Eventually, the Americans decided that he was telling the truth and that the murder of the president had not been organised by the KGB but was, in fact, Oswald acting alone.

Nikita Khrushchev (left) and John F. Kennedy resolved the Cuban Missile Crisis.

The Role of Spies Today

The end of the Cold War brought a change in the way spies operate. In today's world, wars are no longer fought only on the battlefield, but also against extremist groups seeking to carry out terrorist attacks around the world.

Terrorism

Acts of terrorism can be classed as either domestic or international. An example of domestic terrorism, particular to Britain, is the trouble terrorists caused in their bid to split Northern Ireland from the UK and so create a united Ireland.

International Terrorism

In an act of international terrorism, extremist Islamic group Al Qaida attacked Western civilisation by flying two planes into the World Trade Center on 11th September 2001, destroying the twin towers.

A New Era

Terrorism is probably the most urgent and serious problem facing spies today. Spies must use all their wit and skill to infiltrate terrorist groups or trail them to learn their secrets.

The New York skyline is sadly very different today.

The Role of Spies Today

Below is a list from MI5 detailing major terrorist events since the end of the Cold War.

1991 The Provisional IRA (PIRA) attacks Downing Street during a meeting of the Cabinet.

1993 A huge PIRA bomb explodes in Bishopsgate, London, killing two people and causing over £350 million of damage.

1994 PIRA declares a 'cessation of military operations' and Sinn Féin enters the ongoing Northern Ireland peace talks.

1996 After a breakdown in talks, PIRA resumes its attacks in Northern Ireland and the mainland, bombing London's Docklands and Manchester city centre.

1997 PIRA declares a second ceasefire.

Britain's internal espionage services operate from MI5 HQ.

1998 Al Qaida vehicle bombs explode outside United States embassies in Kenya and Tanzania, killing over 220 people and injuring over 4,000 more. In Northern Ireland, 29 people are killed and over 200 injured when the dissident Real IRA attacks Omagh.

2000 The Greek terrorist group November 17 assassinates Brigadier Stephen Saunders, the British military attaché to Greece. The group's leaders are captured and convicted.

2001 Al Qaida operatives attack the World Trade Center and Pentagon using hijacked aircraft, killing themselves and nearly 3,000 other people.

2002 202 people are killed in an Al Qaida-linked attack in Bali, Indonesia.

2004 Terrorists attack Madrid commuter trains, killing 191 people and injuring more than 1,500.

2005 Suicide bombers attack the London transport network, killing 56 people and injuring over 700.

The Babington Plot

The following ten pages take a closer look at some of the most famous spy stories in history, starting with the Babington Plot over 400 years ago.

The Background

In the second half of the 16th century, England was bitterly divided by religion, with the Catholics on one side and the Protestants on the other. The queen, Elizabeth I, was a Protestant, but her cousin and the next in line to the throne, Mary, Queen of Scots, was a Catholic. Many Catholics wanted Mary to be Queen of England immediately and so she was regarded as a threat

This picture shows Mary, Queen of Scots.

by all Elizabeth's supporters and, in particular, her spymaster Francis Walsingham.

Guard

For years Mary was kept under an unusual guard, allowed to hunt and keep staff, but not allowed to move around the country. When Walsingham decided that she was too much of a threat, he sent her to Chartley House, near Sheffield, where she was kept under even closer guard than before.

A portrait of Queen Elizabeth I.

24

Smuggled Letters

Even though her movements were restricted, Mary found she was able to smuggle letters to and from her supporters, including Anthony Babington. Letters written in code were hidden in watertight pouches and then hidden in beer casks sent to and taken from Chartley.

Double Cross

What Mary didn't realise was that she had been set up by Walsingham. He knew that letters were being sent because he had devised the scheme for sending the letters himself. His spies decoded the letters before they were passed on to the intended recipient.

Caught Red-handed

Babington sent Mary a letter detailing how and by whom Elizabeth was to be murdered. Mary would then be freed. When Mary replied to the letter, not disapproving of the plan, it was interpreted that she was plotting against the queen – an offence punishable by death.

Execution

Mary was executed on 8th February 1587, at Fotheringhay Castle in Northamptonshire. Traditionally the executioner would hold up the head of the victim and cry out 'God save the Queen' after the head had been successfully chopped off. When he held up Mary's head, he held it by her hair, not realising it was a wig. To general disgust, the head fell from the wig and rolled across the floor.

Mary smuggled letters to and from her supporters in beer casks.

6 4 7 8 8

The Man Who Never Was

An intelligence trick used by Britain and her Allies in World War Two, 'the man who never was' proved vital to the Allied war effort.

From 1934 until his death in 1945, Adolf Hitler was the leader of Germany.

The Background

Having suffered great losses between 1939 and 1941, the British forces, now receiving the support of the USA, were doing better and had successfully removed German forces from North Africa by the spring of 1943. The time had now come to attack another area held by the Germans. The choice was either Greece or Italy.

Operation Mincemeat

Churchill, the British prime minister, decided that Italy was the better option. But the Allies realised that this was what the Germans would suspect so they set out to deceive them. The plan became known as Operation Mincemeat.

The Deception

A dead body was thrown out to sea on the Spanish coast. The body carried false identification papers indicating that the dead man was Major William Martin of the Royal Marines,

British Prime Minister Winston C...

Louis Mountbatten (left).

a member of Louis Mountbatten's staff. At the time Mountbatten was Commander-in-Chief of the Allied Forces in the Mediterranean.

Coded Letter

A briefcase containing a 'top-secret' letter from one Allied general to another was placed in a waterproof briefcase chained to the body's arm. The coded letter explained that the Allies were hoping to deceive the Germans into thinking that they planned to invade Sicily, an island to the south of Italy, not Greece. Of

Field Marshal Montgomery.

course, the opposite was true. It was a double bluff.

Attention to Detail

The Allies left nothing to chance. Major Martin's personal effects included letters from his father, bank statements and love letters from a girl called Pam. There was even a picture of the girl.

The Operation

A British submarine, *Seraph*, rose to the surface on the Spanish coast and threw out the body, hoping that it would be discovered. The body was picked up by the coastguard, and the Spanish authorities handed over the information to the Germans.

Did it Work?

Files opened after the war showed that the plan had succeeded. Hitler strengthened the German defences in Greece and ignored Sicily. The weakness of German forces there ensured that the Allied troops, led by General Patten and Field Marshal Montgomery, were able to invade Sicily successfully.

The Georgi Markov Affair

Few people would remember Georgi Markov, a Bulgarian politician and writer, were it not for the dramatic circumstances of his murder.

The Background

Bulgaria was occupied by Germany during World War Two, but the Soviet Union successfully invaded the country in 1944, forcing their own political system, communism, on the Bulgarians. People were not allowed to criticise the new system, and would be taking a massive risk if they did.

President Zhivkov.

Georgi Markov.

Danger

Georgi Markov was brave enough to criticise the system and this put him in great danger. In 1969 he escaped from Bulgaria and went to live in London. He worked as a journalist and broadcast anti-communist messages that could be heard in Bulgaria. Thus he had made himself an enemy of both the Bulgarian government, headed by President Zhivkov, and the Soviet Union. The KGB agreed to help the Bulgarians to get rid of Markov, on the condition that their involvement was kept a secret.

Spiked Drink

In spring 1978 a party was held in Markov's honour at Radio Free Europe. A spy put poison in Markov's drink, but he survived as there was not enough poison to kill him. A second attempt to kill him in the summer, while he was on holiday with his family in Sardinia, also failed.

The Fateful Day

On 7th September 1978, Markov was working for the BBC in London. After completing his morning's work he went home for some lunch. For his journey back to the office, he went to catch a bus on the south side of Waterloo Bridge.

The Georgi Markov Affair

A lethal umbrella killed Markov.

The Dropped Umbrella

As Markov approached the bus stop he felt a stinging pain in the back of his right leg. He turned around to see a man bending down to pick up an umbrella. The man apologised to Markov in a foreign accent and then called a taxi. Three days later Markov developed a high fever and died.

Postmortem

As Markov's death was suspicious it was examined in a process called a postmortem. Doctors found a tiny pellet in the wound in the back of his leg. The pellet itself had holes. Further investigation showed that the holes had been filled with ricin, a highly poisonous substance.

Murder Weapon

It was then realised that the umbrella was the murder weapon. The ricin pellet had been held at the tip of the umbrella and the shaft concealed the syringe used to inject the poison.

Guilt

Several years later the KGB admitted they had helped the Bulgarians to kill Markov, but the killer himself was never found.

Waterloo Bridge.

Alexander Litvinenko

In November 2006, Alexander Litvinenko, an ex-Russian secret service recruit living in the UK, was hospitalised. He died three weeks later from rare radiation poisoning, and accusations were made that the Russian government had ordered his death.

Who was Alexander Litvinenko?

Alexander Litvinenko was born in Russia in 1962. He worked for the KGB and its successor, the FSB, but was also a dissident and was arrested after he accused the Russian authorities of ordering an assassination of the Russian billionaire Boris Berezovsky. He was released, and he fled to the UK where he was given protection and became a UK citizen.

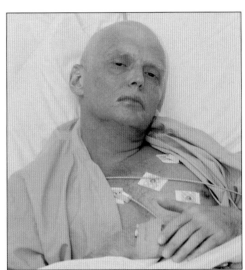

The polonium-210 caused Litvinenko to lose his hair. He was unable to eat and couldn't speak in the days before he died.

Polonium-210

On 1st November 2006 Litvinenko suddenly became ill and was admitted to hospital. After testing, it was discovered that he had significant amounts of a rare toxic element in his body called radionuclide polonium-210. Polonium-210 can cause illness if it is ingested, inhaled or absorbed. He just kept getting sicker, until he eventually died in hospital on 23rd November 2006.

Alexander Litvinenko

Circumstances

Litvinenko said that he had met with three ex-KGB agents on the day that he became ill. He also met with an Italian acquaintance who was involved with investigating KGB intelligence on Italian politics. As a result of this, one of the restaurants that he had visited, a sushi bar, closed for investigation.

Conclusions

On 26th January 2007 British officials said that the murder had been solved. They had searched through all the places Litvinenko had recently been and concluded that the poison had been administered through a teapot by one of the ex-KGB agents he had met on the day he became ill.

Russian Reaction

The British authorities also concluded that Litvinenko's death had been ordered by someone in power. In response, the Russian president, Vladimir Putin, said that the Russian authorities had no need or desire to kill Litvinenko, and that he himself does not believe in conspiracy theories.

What is Polonium-210?

• Polonium-210 was first discovered at the end of the 19th century by Polish-French physicist and chemist Marie Curie, who was a pioneer in the field of radioactivity. In fact, polonium was named in honour of Marie Curie's nationality.

• It is a radioactive material that occurs naturally in very small amounts in the soil and the atmosphere.

• Everyone has a small, safe amount of polonium-210 in their body, but large amounts can cause damage to the body's tissues and organs, as in the case of Alexander Litvinenko.

• Polonium-210 is difficult to obtain and is very hard for doctors to identify. The person that poisoned Litvinenko must have been very skillful, and probably had access to a sophisticated laboratory.

Double Agents

Double agents trade in treachery. Their work is twice as dangerous as that of ordinary spies, and they are in big trouble if caught.

The Cambridge Spies

The Cambridge spies are perhaps the most famous double agents of all time. So named because they had all been to Cambridge University, they were Kim Philby, Guy Burgess, Donald Maclean and Anthony Blunt. They were all recruited to the KGB while students, and only joined British intelligence after they left the university.

Cambridge University.

Kim Philby

Philby was the most important of the Cambridge spies because of the positions he rose to within MI6. Between 1944 and 1946 he was head of a vital counter-espionage department and later operated as the main link between MI6 and the CIA. He was therefore able to pass on both British and American secrets to the Soviets. It was not until 1963, when he fled to the Soviet Union, that it was discovered he was a double agent.

Burgess and Maclean

Burgess and Maclean worked in less important positions in British intelligence although Maclean did rise to be head of the American department of the Foreign Office. They both fled to Russia in 1951, having been warned by Philby that they were about to be caught.

Below: Guy Burgess. Right: Donald Maclean.

It was suspected at the time that it must have been Philby who warned them, but somehow he got away with it.

Blunt

Blunt confessed to being a double agent in 1964, on the condition that he would not be sent to prison. His treacherous work had involved helping to recruit other agents to the KGB and passing information to the Russian government. Astonishingly, he was allowed to continue in his role as Surveyor of the Queen's Pictures. His knighthood, which he had been awarded in 1956, was taken away in 1979.

Aldrich Ames

American double agent Aldrich Ames began his spying career after being appointed head of the CIA's Russian counter-intelligence division in 1985. Short of money following his divorce, he went to the KGB offering secrets in return for payment. Over the next ten years he revealed the names of CIA agents in Russia. Many of these agents were then shot by the Russians. When Ames was finally caught he was sentenced to life imprisonment.

Anthony Blunt – surveyor of the Queen's pictures until 1972.

Tailing & Tracking

Following a target has long been a part of a spy's training, and many different techniques are used.

Do you think you could spot someone tailing you?

On Foot

A spy undertakes lots of preparation work before tailing a target. Discovering the target's usual haunts is key to making more detailed plans before carrying out an undercover operation. Getting to know the area, or field, is also important and could prove vital if a backup plan needed to be put into action quickly.

Positioning

Once a target's routine is known, a spy must decide how best to make his or her observations, such as taking photographs and making detailed notes. It may be that surveillance from a hotel room or private house, for example, works best, or a spy may choose to wear a disguise and follow the target discreetly.

Cover Story

As well as wearing a disguise appropriate to the surroundings, a spy often needs to conceal his or her true identity. A false ID, passport or birth certificate, for example, could prove vital to a spy if caught. Other props, such as a dog lead, may also help a spy explain his or her presence. The simplest props arouse the least suspicion!

From the seismic intruder of the Cold War era to the tracing of mobile phone signals today, tracking a target's movements is made easier through technology.

Seismic Intruder

Designed to blend in with its surroundings, the seismic intruder detection device is capable of detecting any movement, be it people, animals or objects, up to 300 metres away. The device has a built-in transmitter, which relays its findings back to base. A spy would hide the device in an appropriate spot – disguised as a stone and hidden amongst vegetation, for example – and then return to the safety of the base to gather evidence of the target's activity.

Mobile Tracking

Think a mobile phone is private? Think again! Since mobile phones send out constant radio transmitting signals, anyone with the right technology can put a trace on a mobile number and know the target's exact position in minutes!

Today's hand-held Global Positioning Systems (GPS) mean that spies will find it easier to get around in unfamiliar places.

Bugging

Being able to listen in on conversations has provided spies with very valuable information they could not get any other way.

Recorded Radio

Traditionally a spy could install a bug in a telephone receiver, briefcase, dashboard of a car – anywhere where they thought it might pick up the information they needed. The spy would then set up a radio nearby, with a machine for recording broadcasts attached, so that hours of data could be saved and evidence recorded.

Belly Buster

The Belly Buster was a hand-operated drill used to make holes in walls and pillars. The holes would then be filled with listening devices. Of course, the Belly Buster was designed to be used silently. The spy would have to hold the base of the drill against their stomach to stifle noise while the drill was powered by a handle that was turned manually.

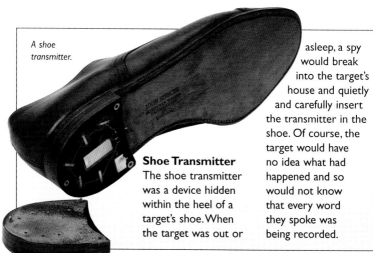

A shoe transmitter.

Shoe Transmitter

The shoe transmitter was a device hidden within the heel of a target's shoe. When the target was out or asleep, a spy would break into the target's house and quietly and carefully insert the transmitter in the shoe. Of course, the target would have no idea what had happened and so would not know that every word they spoke was being recorded.

Mobile Phones

Since some mobile phone microphones can be turned on remotely, even when the phones themselves are switched off, intelligence services are able to listen in on private conversations. A mobile phone can be reprogrammed using wireless technology, so the owner's conversation can be transmitted without their knowledge!

Laser Microphone

Although they cost a lot and are difficult to use, laser microphones have been in use since the Cold War. A laser beam is bounced off an object close to where a conversation is being held. The sound of the conversation makes the object vibrate. Another device is then used to translate the vibrations into the eavesdropped conversation!

Trojan Horses

Now that the Internet is so widely used, one of the best ways to bug a target is through his or her computer. The most commonly used method of doing this is with a programme called a Trojan Horse. A Trojan Horse is smuggled onto a computer, usually inside another programme, and is activated when the target downloads a game or opens an application, for example. Once the Trojan Horse has been installed by the unsuspecting target, all the files on the target's computer can be accessed.

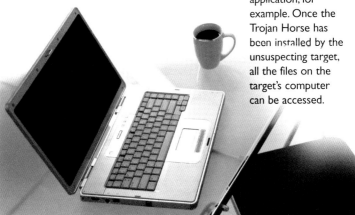

Wireless technology has made computer hacking easier to carry out.

Secret Messages

Spies have been using codes for centuries to hide information from their enemies. The Internet has made hidden messages almost impossible to find!

Code Words

Spies often have their own language. This means they can use normal methods of communication, such as telephones, to relay top secret information – even if they are being bugged, no one outside their group will know what they are talking about! Often spy groups will regularly change the most sensitive code words to avoid detection. Some commonly used spy words are explained in the box below.

Encryption

Information sent via the Internet, and even the information on a computer, can be protected from anyone seeing it by using encryption methods. Email is encrypted using a system of public-key cryptography, where a public and a private key or formula are used to encode a message. To decode it, a person would need to know both keys, but the private one is hidden!

Encryption uses large random numbers to keep information secure.

SPY TALK!

Watcher – A surveillance spy
Legend – The background cover story of an undercover agent
Cobbler – A spy who makes false passports
Dead Drop – A place where information can be left for another spy
Safe House – A building used to meet agents
Filling – Putting material in a Dead Drop
Mole – An undercover agent who has penetrated a target's group

---

Hidden Net

Although encryption is widely used to protect the information sent via email, anyone spying on a computer can see that information has been sent and can try to find ways of getting access to that information. Obviously, the perfect way to pass on a secret message is to make sure there is no trace of it ever being sent. The Internet has made this very easy to do. Pictures can be posted in a large number of places and will look very innocent. These pictures, however, could contain hidden messages. This method of sending secret messages is called picture steganography. (Turn to page 42 to find out more!)

Old Fashioned?

If a spy suspects enemy agents are watching, then it's likely that his or her phone will be bugged and satellites could be recording every meeting. How tempting would it be for the spy to try the old-fashioned method of passing information by arranging to drop a coded note into a bin as if it were rubbish?

Satellites today can read newspapers from space!

Data Smuggling

Over the years, spies have had to think of all sorts of creative ways to conceal top secret information!

Tiny Data

Storing data in secret places has been a key part of spy training. Information has been gathered and hidden in all sorts of ways, from voice records to pictures and writing. A spy has to be able to collect and smuggle often large amounts of top secret data from right beneath the enemy's nose!

The Voice Pen

The voice pen is a very sophisticated device – it uses a tiny microphone to pick up clearly any sounds around it. The information is stored on disks, which are then read by a computer. By using computers, hours of conversation can be quickly scanned for evidence.

Dead Drop Spike

The dead drop spike (above) is one of the tools of the trade for a spy travelling to a dead drop. The spike, big enough to conceal money, maps and secret documents, is hidden in the dead drop area. The spike is waterproof and so can be hidden in water or soft ground.

Silver Dollar Hollow Container

The silver dollar hollow container is a great spying device. Designed to look like an ordinary coin it is, in fact, hollow. Agents can pass coins to one another without attracting suspicion. Of course, the coins conceal secret messages!

The silver dollar hollow container looks like ordinary pocket change.

RFID Tags

RFID (Radio-Frequency Identification) tags are tiny devices that can be attached to an object, implanted into an animal or even put under the skin of a human.

Data can be programmed onto an RFID tag so that whatever it is attached to can carry information discreetly.

RFID tags are an ever-growing technology and have many uses, such as tracking animals and preventing car crime.

RFID technology is also now used by many countries in passports.

These identification documents have a tiny data storage containing the holder's personal details along with a digital photo. The tags are able to record the travel history of the holder – date, time and place of exit and entry, for example – making it easier for spies to track known targets.

A USB Memory Stick is able to hold a large amount of information.

Memory Sticks

For a spy, being able to hold a large amount of information on a tiny device is invaluable, as they often have to smuggle data in and out of countries. In 1998 Sony released the Memory Stick, a tiny card that could hold 128MB of information. Technology moves quickly, and in 2006 a new Memory Stick was unveiled that could hold 8GB – over sixty times bigger than the original card!

Steganography

Writing hidden messages that only the recipient will be able to decipher is known as steganography. The word 'steganography' comes from the Greek words meaning 'covered, or hidden, writing'.

Ancient Greece

Steganography can be traced to ancient Greece of the 5th century BC. Greek historian Herodotus recorded two examples. The first tells of a warning about a planned attack on Greece and was concealed beneath the wax of a wooden tablet. The second example is where the head of a trusted slave was shaved and a message tattooed on it. Once the slave's hair grew back, the message was hidden and the slave was able to deliver it in safety and without arousing suspicion. Steganographic techniques have developed with technology and are still in use today.

Picture Steganography

Digital pictures are the perfect medium in which to hide messages, since they use a large amount of data themselves. If you took a digital photo of a tree, for example, you would see many shades of green and brown in the picture. However, the differences between some of the shades will be impossible to see with the human eye. A computer, on the other hand, will be able to register these subtle changes. It is within these tiny, unseen differences that data can be hidden. It is even possible to hide a completely different picture within the first!

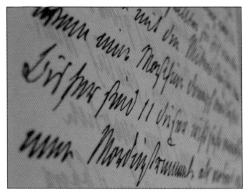

Data is an easy tool for concealing secret messages.

Terrorist Weapon?

In the last few years, several newspapers have reported that terrorists are using steganography to send hidden messages to other members of their groups via the Internet. Security experts have been unable to find any evidence that this is the case, but with so many images posted on the Internet every day, it is impossible to rule it out. With terrorism becoming international, terrorists need to find ways to pass secret messages to associates all over the world. Can you think of a better way to do this than over the Internet?

How to Fight Steganography!

To find out if a picture has been encoded with secret data, a process called steganalysis is used. To do this, an original of the picture that is thought to have been tampered with is compared with the sent picture. A picture can also be compressed, which will limit the amount of data used to make it, and therefore make any unusual aspects of the picture visible. For steganalysis to work, however, you need to be able to identify a picture for examination in the first place!

The second picture was hidden in the first!

Industrial Espionage

When one company wants to gain advantage over a competitor, it may try to find out information the other company doesn't want it to know. If the method used is illegal, it's called industrial espionage.

Two Ways

There are two main ways in which companies go in for industrial espionage – angry workers or sleepers.

Angry Worker

If a worker doesn't like the company that employs them, they may decide to hurt the company's business. This is called sabotage. As long as nobody suspects that the worker doesn't enjoy their job, it will be very easy for them to gain access to passwords, security codes and top-secret computer files. Some companies will watch the workers at their rival company carefully, in the hope of finding one angry worker they can persuade to work for them.

Sleeper

Other companies use workers trained not to attract suspicion. Their workers get jobs in the target company's organisation and then regularly feed information to their original employer.

Sleepers pass information to people who pay them.

Industrial Espionage

Although the spies will be in a lot of trouble when they're caught, until then they are being paid by two companies. If the sleeper is a computer programmer, he or she may be able to write a programme called a 'Trojan Horse' into the company's computer network (see page 37), allowing remote access to computer data.

Industrial espionage can be risky for those involved.

Computers

Nowadays, the workplace is dominated by computers, which hold vital information about individual companies. There are some people who are able to use one computer to find out the information stored on another. These people are called hackers.

Fierce Competition!

In the technological world of gaming, having an advantage over your competitors means everything – you would not want them learning about your latest invention and copying it! Devices such as the latest console, for example, are eagerly awaited and surrounded in mystery. Even when new games are shown at exhibitions before a console is released, they will be shown on 'devkits' rather than the actual console itself. These companies do everything in their power to make sure their competitors don't know of their latest technological developments!

Counterintelligence is used to frustrate the enemy. This can take many forms.

False Feed

As a spy, once you've trapped an enemy agent, you turn the tables on your opponent by not revealing that you now know someone is working against you. Instead, you feed false information to the enemy agent in the hope that he or she will pass on misleading information.

Using CCTV to monitor people's movements.

CCTV is commonly used as a security measure.

CCTV

Of course, counter-intelligence is not just about cross and double cross. There is also surveillance. CCTV (closed circuit television) is commonly used as a security measure. Everything that happens within the camera's view is relayed back to agents who can watch what is happening without people realising that they can be seen.

Counterintelligence

Satellites

Satellites can be used for military purposes. They are used to record images of a particular area of interest to an intelligence agency. A recent invention is the tiny picosatellite, which weighs less than one kilogramme. It is so small that hundreds of them can be launched into space at a time. Its size means that it can be rapidly deployed to cover a particular area of interest.

Bug Sweeping

Bug sweeping involves making regular searches for spying devices and updating security measures. Bugs may be hidden in a number of places – in a phone receiver or plant pot, for example – and tiny cameras may be hidden in walls or ceilings. Computer password keys and keys to secret codes should all be changed regularly.

Handle Carefully

If bugs are found, they should be handled very carefully. They may reveal fingerprints or DNA evidence that could lead to the spy who installed the surveillance equipment.

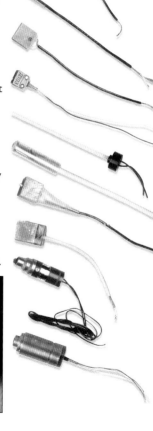

A selection of bugging devices.

A satellite can be used to transmit images, which can be used to aid spies.

Glossary

CIA Criminal Intelligence Agency, responsible for US intelligence abroad.

Communism political system used to rule the Soviet Union from 1917 to 1990.

Counterintelligence spying on an enemy's spies.

Double agent pretending to spy for one country but really spying for another.

Industrial espionage spying for a company.

Encryption putting a message into code.

Enigma machine used to encode German naval communications in World War Two.

False feed giving untrue information to a known spy in the hope that they will pass it on.

FBI Federal Bureau of Investigation, responsible for American domestic security.

FSB replacement for the KGB.

Hacker a person who can break through the security codes of a computer.

KGB Committee of State Security, responsible for Soviet Union espionage.

Lorenz machine used to encode communications between Germany's top generals in World War Two.

Manhattan Project top-secret project led by Britain and the USA to develop a nuclear bomb.

MI5 organisation that looks after British domestic security.

MI6 organisation that spies for Britain abroad.

Minutemen volunteer soldiers who fought for the USA during the War of Independence.

Mossad Israeli secret service.

NKVD precursor to the KGB.

Sleeper a spy planted in advance for future use.

Stasi secret police in East Germany.

Trojan Horse device used by computer programmers to allow remote access to a computer's data at will.